I0798832

Contents

SRA Early Interventions in Reading

NOMADS: People on the Move

By Chandler Tyrrell

McGraw Hill Education

Photo Credits: Cover, Back Cover © McGraw-Hill Education/Barry Barker

mheducation.com/prek-12

McGraw-Hill Education

Send all inquiries to:
McGraw-Hill Education
8787 Orion Place
Columbus, OH 43240

ISBN: 978-0-07-604468-9
MHID: 0-07-604468-8

Printed in the United States of America.

16 17 18 19 20 MER 28 27 26 25

Chapter 1
The Changpa

Early humans did not know how to cultivate crops or how to raise animals for food. In order to survive, they roamed from place to place to find food. They hunted animals and found berries and plants to eat. Eventually, humans learned how to cultivate crops and how to raise animals on farms for food. Cities formed near farms, and people began to stay in one place. Today, most people move only a few times in their lifetimes.

Yet there are still some people in the world who move a lot from place to place. These people are nomads. Nomads do not have just one home. They live in different places at different times of the year. Each group of nomads continues to move around for different reasons.

The Changpa are nomads in India in the Himalayas. The Himalayas are mountains. The Changpa have learned how to raise animals and herd goats, sheep, and yaks. These animals graze, which means they eat grass. But grass doesn't grow well in the mountains; the ground is rocky and dry. So even though the Changpa have learned how to raise animals, they still need to move around frequently, looking for new grazing grass.

Yak hair helps the Changpa in many ways. The Changpa live in *rebos,* which are tents woven from yak hair. Yak hair is also used to make carpets and ropes, and yak milk is used to make cheese, yogurt, and butter. Yak droppings are burned to make fires for cooking and heating. Yaks also help the Changpa move by carrying overweight things on their backs from place to place.

Changpa sheep have wool called cashmere. After the wool has been cut off the sheep, the Changpa people travel to the city to sell the wool at the markets for money. Then the Changpa go back into the mountains to travel again. People buy the wool to weave into blankets and clothing that are of great value.

Chapter 2

The Machiguenga

The Machiguenga live in Manu National Park in Peru. Some of them live outside the park and work for wood, oil, or coffee companies. Others continue to live the way the Machiguenga people have lived for hundreds of years. The Machiguenga are nomads who hunt, fish, and cultivate crops.

Manu National Park is a huge area. Rain forest covers most of the park, and there are many writhing rivers. The Machiguenga people set up their towns near the rivers and streams in the forest so they have a way to travel. They use the water to float boats and travel places.

Machiguenga families have more than one home because of the wet and dry seasons. Families live one place during the wet season when it rains a lot, which helps their crops grow. The biggest crop is manioc. It's like a potato. During the dry season when it doesn't rain as much and the Machiguenga's food and crops won't grow, they live in towns where there are schools for children to learn to read and write.

During the dry season when the rivers are low, the Machiguenga move again to another neighborhood. Families camp along these rivers, where fish are easier to catch, and turtle eggs can be found in the soil. When the dry season ends, it's time to move back to the town near the schools for children to learn to read and write. Later, the Machiguenga will move back to their farms during the wet season.

In order to cultivate crops, part of the forest has to be cut and burned to make a field. This isn't wrong—burning the soil actually makes the soil healthy because it replaces nutrients that help plants grow. After two or three years, the soil is no longer healthy and cannot grow any more crops. The Machiguenga have to make a new field in another place.

Women work in the fields during the wet season. They use their hands and wrists to gather and load up wild fruits and nuts from the forest for food. One popular snack is ice-cream beans. They are sweet white nuts. Beetle grubs are also eaten. People say they taste like peanut butter! While the women farm, the men hunt for meat or fish.

Chapter 3

The Nenetses

In the far north of Russia in Siberia, the Nenetses travel across the tundra. Tundra is found in the coldest parts of the world. Very few trees or plants grow there because the tundra ground is frozen most of the year. The Nenetses move as the seasons change because the location of the best food for their reindeer changes with the seasons.

Reindeer are very important to the Nenets people. Reindeer give the people many things of value that help them live. Warm clothing and tents called *chums* are made from reindeer skin. The Nenetses also get most of what they eat from the reindeer, by using many parts of the reindeer.

In the summer, the tundra is not as cold, and the reindeer like to eat lichen, which is like a plant and grows on the tundra's rocks. Reindeer have special hooves like sharp, thick toenails. The hooves help dig into ice to keep the reindeer from slipping on the frozen tundra ground as they search for lichen. There are hundreds of reindeer, and all the lichen in an area is eaten in a short time. Then the Nenetses must roam to a new area.

The *chums* the Nenetses live in look like tepees. Inside, a wood fire burns. Furs are on the *chum* walls and keep out the cold. Nenetses drink hot tea to keep themselves warm. The tea is made from loads of clean, melted snow.

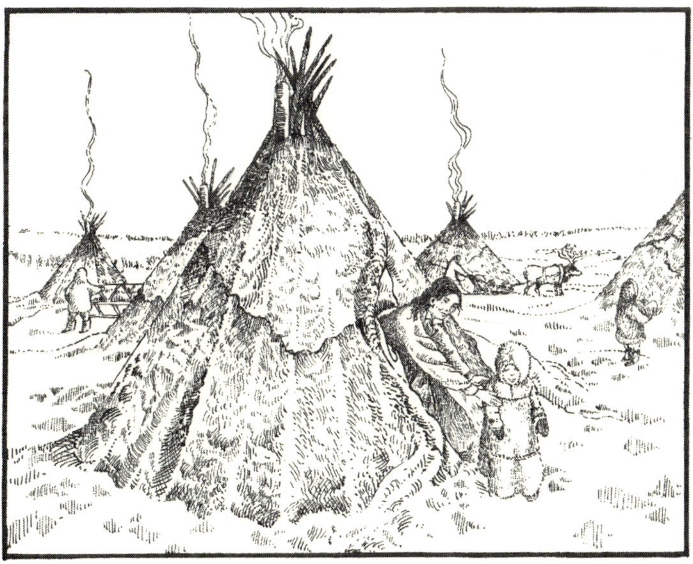

When winter arrives, the Nenets nomads move south. They take down their camp and then wrap it up and put everything in the camp onto wooden sleds. Reindeer pull the weight on the sleds to warmer places. In the south, the tundra has more trees. This area also has animals and plants for the Nenetses.

When the adults move south in winter with the reindeer, the children stay behind to go to school. Some children also visit parts of the world that have telephones and electricity, but most choose to remain where they were born and continue living the life of the nomad.

Chapter 4

The Bedouins

Bedouins live in the desert and travel in some of the driest arid lands on Earth. They move across the Arabian and North African deserts. These Arab nomads survive by herding camels, goats, and sheep. Bedouins roam in search of water and good grazing areas. In this harsh land, such an oasis is very hard to find.

Bedouins wear long, loose robes. They wrap scarves around their heads and faces. Their clothes keep away the hot sun and the strong winds of the desert. Bedouin tents are partly made of goat or camel hair. Inside the tents, Bedouins stay cool during the summer and warm during the winter.

During the hottest part of summer, Bedouin families stay in one place because it's too hot and too risky to cross the desert. Some families live in cities because they want to be near water. But when the weather gets cooler, Bedouins load up their things and move across the desert as they have always done.

Each Bedouin group travels inside its own large area. Piles of stones mark a group's land. Bedouins watch for the piles and don't travel into another group's area. This way, Bedouins respect each other's privacy and land.

Camels are the Bedouins' most important animals. Camels can go days without water in the desert and can carry a lot of weight too.

Life in the desert is difficult, and Bedouins are usually one of the only groups of people living there. For this reason, Bedouins don't meet other travelers very often. If Bedouins do have visitors to their camp, they treat the visitors as special guests and invite them inside their tents. The Bedouins give their guests tea, coffee, and food. Bedouins are good hosts and remain friendly even in the harsh desert.

Chapter 5

The Masai

The Masai people live on the plains of the African savanna. A savanna is an area that is covered in grass. The Masai have lived in this grassland for hundreds of years. They are nomads who travel with herds of cows. The Masai roam across the land, looking for the best grazing spots.

A Masai town is called an *enkang.* The houses in the town are placed in a circle. The houses are shaped a little like igloos. Masai women make the houses from things found in the savanna: sticks, grass, and cow droppings. There are piles of thorns around the town to keep out foes and wild animals.

The savanna has many grassy plains. But if the Masai stay in one place too long, woefully their cows eat all the grass. The Masai must move to a new area so that the plains they leave behind have a chance to grow back. The Masai can return after the grass has grown again.

The Masai women and girls work in the town while the Masai men and boys herd the animals. Animals are a very important part of the Masai way of life. The Masai get milk and meat from their animals. The Masai also sell their animals to other people to get money.

The Masai herd goats and sheep. They used to trade these animals with others, but cows are now the most important animals. Today the Masai sometimes sell cows for money. The more animals a family has, the more money the family gets. Selling cows for money is changing the way the families live.

Like all nomads, the Masai have less and less land to live on, because the modern world is using the land for other things. Much Masai land has been made into parks. People also approach and search for oil in the ground there. Woefully, the way of life for many nomads is ending.